Spooky Jokes for Funny Kids

BUSTER BOOKS

Illustrated by
Andrew Pinder

Compiled and edited by Caroline Rowlands
Designed by Jilly Slattery

Manufacturer: First published in Great Britain in 2025 by Buster Books, an imprint of Michael O'Mara Books Limited, 9 Lion Yard, Tremadoc Road, London SW4 7NQ
www.mombooks.com

Represented by: Authorised Rep Compliance Ltd, Ground Floor, 71 Lower Baggot Street, Dublin D02 P593, Ireland
www.arccompliance.com

 www.mombooks.com/buster
 Buster Books
 @buster_books

Copyright © Buster Books 2025

All rights reserved. You may not copy, store, distribute, transmit, reproduce or otherwise make available this publication (or any part of it) in any form, or by any means (electronic, digital, optical, mechanical, photocopying, recording, machine readable, text/data mining or otherwise), without the prior written permission of the publisher. Any person who does any unauthorized act in relation to this publication may be liable to criminal prosecution and civil claims for damages.

A CIP catalogue record for this book is available from the British Library.

ISBN: 978-1-83725-103-2

1 3 5 7 9 10 8 6 4 2

This product is made of material from well-managed, FSC®-certified forests and other controlled sources. The manufacturing processes conform to the environmental regulations of the country of origin.

Printed and bound in August 2025 by CPI Group (UK) Ltd, Croydon, CR0 4YY.

MIX
Paper | Supporting responsible forestry
FSC® C013604

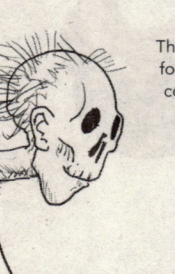

For further information see www.mombooks.com/about/sustainability-climate-focus
Report any safety issues to product.safety@mombooks.com

CONTENTS

Spooky Sniggers	5
Witchy Wonders	18
Ghostly Gags	30
Gory Gastro Guffaws	43
Halloween Howlers	53
Skeleton Snorters	66
Monster Marvels	76
Knock, Knock, Boo!	91
Creepy Creatures	101
Terrifying Ticklers	117

Introduction

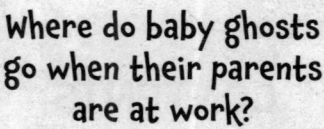

Where do baby ghosts go when their parents are at work?

Day scare.

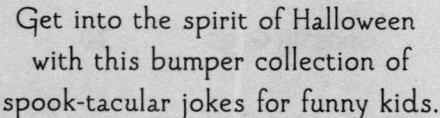

Get into the spirit of Halloween with this bumper collection of spook-tacular jokes for funny kids.

In this book you will find over 300 terrifying ticklers, from ghostly gags and witchy wonders to hilarious Halloween howlers. Share the funniest with your friends and family to get them cackling all spooky season.

If these don't tickle your funny bone, then nothing will!

SPOOKY JOKES FOR FUNNY KIDS

Which play is most popular with monsters?

Romeo and Ghouliet.

Why did the zombie go to school?

He wanted to improve his deaducation.

Why do vampires brush their teeth a lot?

Because they have bat breath.

SPOOKY JOKES FOR FUNNY KIDS

What position do ghosts love to play in hockey?

Ghoul-keeper.

What do ghosts use to wash their hair?

Sham-BOO.

Why do zombies sleep a lot?

Because they're dead tired.

SPOOKY JOKES FOR FUNNY KIDS

Which dog breed do ghosts like best?

BOO-dles.

Which dog breed do vampires have as pets?

Bloodhounds.

Which snack do panda ghosts love to eat?

Bam-BOO.

SPOOKY JOKES FOR FUNNY KIDS

What do you get if you cross a witch with a hot day?

A sunny spell.

What music do mummies love?

Wrap.

What do you call a ghost who never laughs?

Dead serious.

SPOOKY JOKES FOR FUNNY KIDS

Where do ghosts go to send their mail?

The ghost office.

How does a ghost sneeze?

Ah, ah, ah BOO!

What kind of street does a zombie live in?

A dead end.

Why don't vampires eat cows?

They don't like stakes.

Why did the vampire need a drink?

He was bloodthirsty.

Why did the vampire fail his art exam?

He only knew how to draw blood.

SPOOKY JOKES FOR FUNNY KIDS

Which vampire is the best at arithmetic?

Count Dracula.

Where does a vampire keep his money?

In a blood bank.

Did you hear about the vampire with only one fang?

He just had to grin and bear it.

SPOOKY JOKES FOR FUNNY KIDS

What do you call a zombie who loves to clean?

A grim sweeper.

Why was the ghost scared to go on stage?

In case he got BOOed.

Why don't mummies make good friends?

They're too wrapped up in themselves.

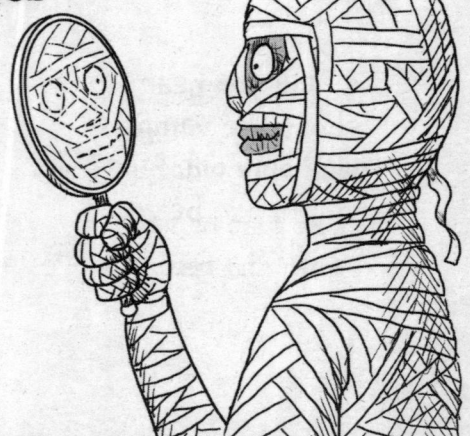

SPOOKY JOKES FOR FUNNY KIDS

What do you get when you cross a vampire and a snowman?

Frostbite.

Why did the vampire go to see the doctor?

Because of his coffin.

What fruit do vampires like best?

Neck-tarines.

SPOOKY JOKES FOR FUNNY KIDS

What do witches in Australia ride around on?

Broom-erangs.

What do you call witches who live together?

Broom-mates.

Why was the witch's broom late?

It over swept.

SPOOKY JOKES FOR FUNNY KIDS

What did the referee say during the witches' baseball game?

No charm, no foul.

Why wouldn't the witch's cat join in with the baseball game?

It was in a bad MEWWWd.

Why do the witches always lose at baseball?

Their bats fly away.

SPOOKY JOKES FOR FUNNY KIDS

Why do witches love to stay in hotels?

Because of the broom service.

What do witches use to do their hair?

Scare spray.

How do you make a witch scratch?

Take away the w.

What do you call it when a witch dreams of winning the lottery?

Witchful thinking.

What happened to the naughty witch at school?

She was ex-spelled.

Why did the witch try so hard at school?

She wanted to be witch and famous.

SPOOKY JOKES FOR FUNNY KIDS

What's a witch's best subject in school?

Spelling!

What do student witches take at the end of the school year?

Hex-ams.

Why did the witch not graduate with the rest of her class?

She was a late broomer.

SPOOKY JOKES FOR FUNNY KIDS

Why did the witch call the plumber?

Hubble bubble toilet trouble.

What do witches love to wear on their wrists?

Charm bracelets.

Why did the witch put her broom in the dishwasher?

She wanted a clean sweep.

SPOOKY JOKES FOR FUNNY KIDS

Why did the witches go on a picnic?

They wanted to enjoy the sunny spell.

What do witches do when they see a shooting star?

Make a witch.

Where do witches bake their cookies?

In a coven.

SPOOKY JOKES FOR FUNNY KIDS

Did you hear about the witch who became a millionaire?

It was a rags to witches story.

What do witches do at the market?

They haggle.

How do witches like their eggs?

Terror-fried.

SPOOKY JOKES FOR FUNNY KIDS

What do you call a ghost in a fireplace?

A toasty ghostie.

What do baby ghosts wear on their feet?

BOO-ties.

What do you get if you cross a chicken and a ghost?

A poultry-geist.

SPOOKY JOKES FOR FUNNY KIDS

Which recipe do all ghosts know how to make?

Ghoulash.

Why did the ghost hate getting caught in the rain?

It dampens her spirit.

Which dessert do ghosts like best?

BOO-noffie pie.

SPOOKY JOKES FOR FUNNY KIDS

What did the witch say to the ghost?

Get a life!

How does a ghost unlock their front door?

With a spoo-key.

Which room in a house will a ghost never enter?

The living room.

SPOOKY JOKES FOR FUNNY KIDS

Why do ghosts love going up in an elevator?

It lifts their spirits.

Does this sheet suit me?

You look BOO-tiful.

Where do ghosts buy their clothes?

At a BOO-tique!

SPOOKY JOKES FOR FUNNY KIDS

What did the skeleton shout after scoring a goal?

GHOOOOOOOOUL!

How did the witch know the ghost was lying?

She could see right through him.

What do ghost pirates search for?

Hidden BOO-ty.

SPOOKY JOKES FOR FUNNY KIDS

Which fairground ride is most popular with ghosts?

The roller-ghoster.

Which ride do all the little ghosts like to go on?

The scary-go-round.

What medicine do ghosts take for colds?

Coffin drops.

SPOOKY JOKES FOR FUNNY KIDS

Which type of tree does a ghost like best?

A ceme-tree!

Why do skeletons think they're better than ghosts?

Because ghosts are so BOO-ring!

I love astrology.

Me too, I always read my horror-scope.

SPOOKY JOKES FOR FUNNY KIDS

What happened to the ghost who got lost in the fog?

He was mist.

What did the granny ghost say to her grandkids?

Do not spook unless you are spooken to.

What did the ghost teacher tell the class?

Look at the board and I'll go through it again.

SPOOKY JOKES FOR FUNNY KIDS

Which musical do ghosts love?

The Phantom of the Opera.

What do you give a ghost with bad eyesight?

Spooktacles.

What did the ghost say when she hit the dancefloor?

Let's BOO-gie on down.

SPOOKY JOKES FOR FUNNY KIDS

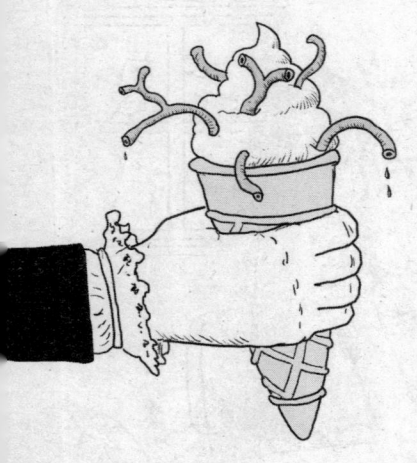

What type of ice cream do vampires love best?

Vein-illa.

What do skeletons love to cook on the BBQ?

Spare ribs.

Why was the werewolf arrested at the butcher's store?

It was chop-lifting.

SPOOKY JOKES FOR FUNNY KIDS

Which monster ate the three bears' porridge?

Ghouldilocks.

What kind of bobbing apple is bad tempered?

A crab apple.

What does a vampire never order with his pizza?

Garlic bread.

SPOOKY JOKES FOR FUNNY KIDS

What kind of treat is never on time for Halloween?

Choco-late.

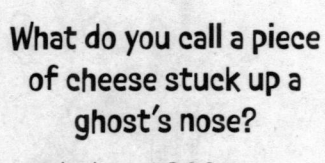

Why is the witch's frog always happy?

It eats whatever bugs it.

What do you call a piece of cheese stuck up a ghost's nose?

A cheese BOO-ger.

SPOOKY JOKES FOR FUNNY KIDS

Where do ghosts buy their food?

The ghostery store.

Why didn't the vampire's cake rise?

He'd made a grave error.

What do polite monsters say at meal times?

Pleased to eat you.

SPOOKY JOKES FOR FUNNY KIDS

What do ghosts put on their crackers?

Scream cheese.

Why didn't the skeleton order spicy food?

He didn't have the stomach for it.

What does a skeleton say before dinner?

Bone appetite!

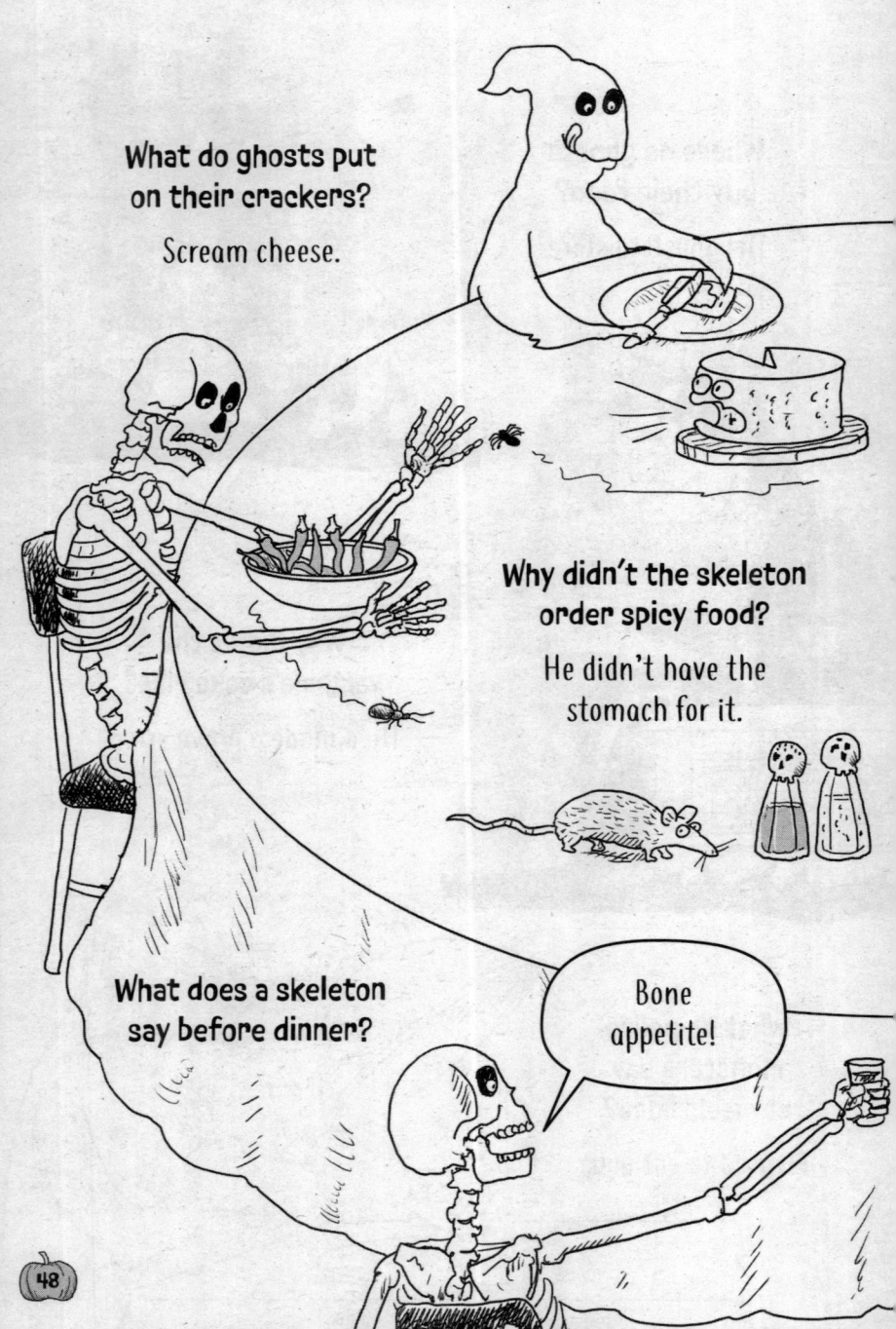

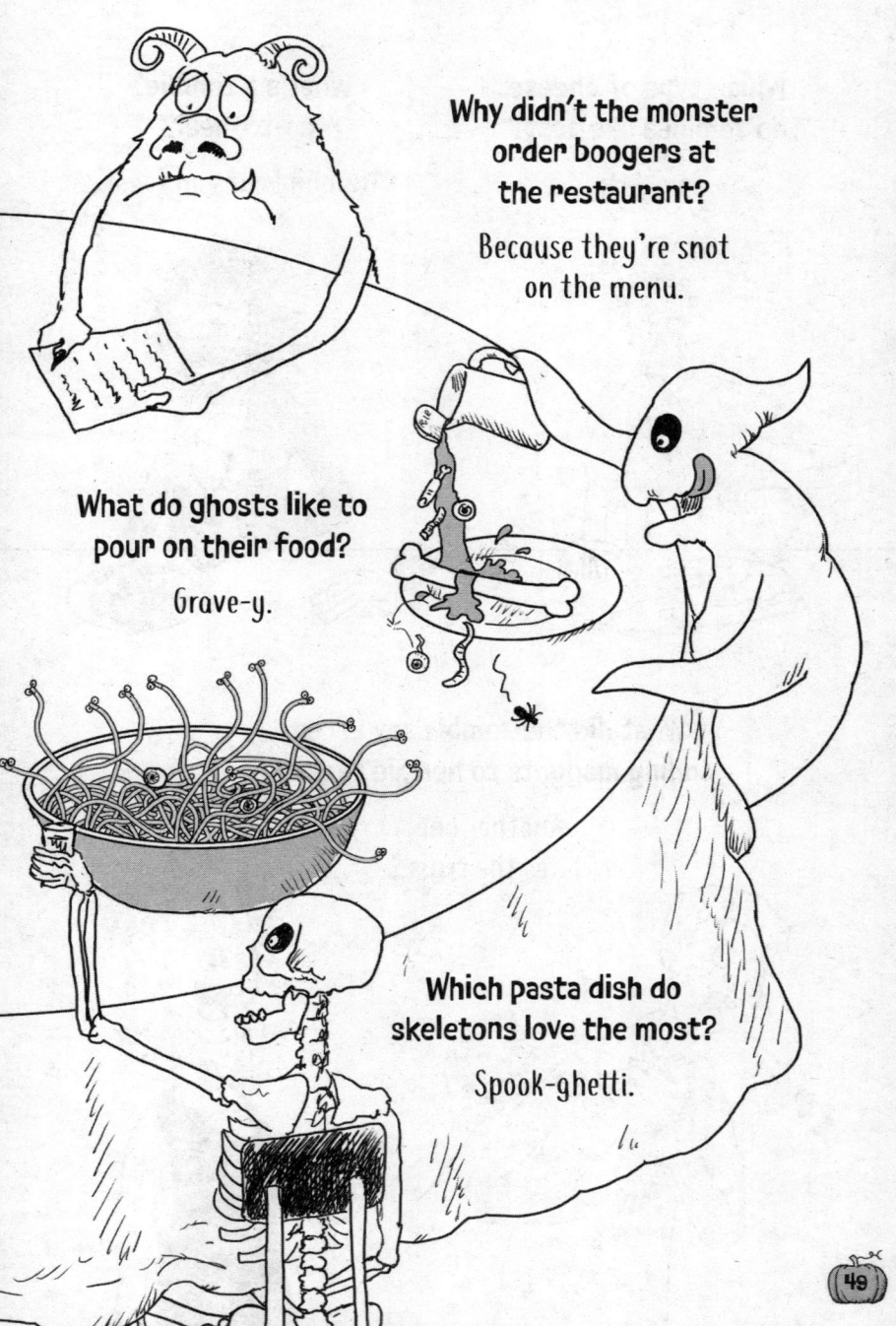

SPOOKY JOKES FOR FUNNY KIDS

Which type of cheese do zombies like best?

Zom-brie.

What's a zombie's go-to meal?

Human beans on toast.

What did the zombie say after adding maggots to her pie recipe?

Another one bites the crust.

SPOOKY JOKES FOR FUNNY KIDS

On which day do monsters eat the most?

Chewsday.

What do you call a chubby jack-o'-lantern?

A plumpkin.

What's a witch's top snack?

A sandwitch.

SPOOKY JOKES FOR FUNNY KIDS

Why was the little skeleton scared to go trick or treating?

It didn't have the guts.

What happens if you throw a boomerang at a ghost on Halloween?

It will come back to haunt you.

What did the monster do when the zombie rolled its eyes at him?

He just rolled them right back.

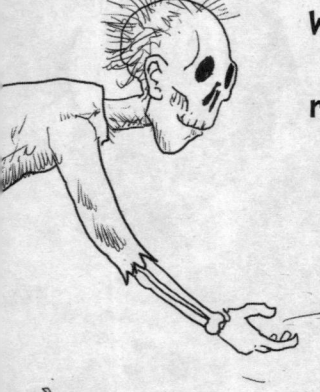

SPOOKY JOKES FOR FUNNY KIDS

When do zombies finish trick or treating?

When they are dead tired.

How do vampires travel around on Halloween?

By blood vessel.

How did the zombie get so good at trick or treating?

Dead-ication.

SPOOKY JOKES FOR FUNNY KIDS

What do owls say when they go trick or treating?

Happy Owl-oween.

What do jack-o'-lanterns say when they set out for trick or treating?

Let's get glowing.

How did the skeleton know it was going to rain on Halloween?

She felt it in her bones.

SPOOKY JOKES FOR FUNNY KIDS

Why did nobody ever invite Dracula trick or treating?

Because he was a pain in the neck.

Why doesn't Dracula eat a lot of Halloween treats?

He's afraid of tooth decay.

Who gives Dracula the most treats on Halloween?

His fang-club.

SPOOKY JOKES FOR FUNNY KIDS

Knock, knock!

Who's there?

Ooze.

Ooze who?

Ooze that monster over there?

Knock, knock!

Who's there?

Woo!

Woo who?

Yeah, I'm excited for Halloween, too!

Knock, knock!

Who's there?

Diane.

Diane who?

Diane to eat my Halloween treats.

SPOOKY JOKES FOR FUNNY KIDS

Knock, knock!

Who's there?

Imogen.

Imogen who?

Imogen Halloween without trick or treating?

Knock, knock!

Who's there?

Gladys.

Gladys who?

Gladys Halloween.

Knock, knock!

Who's there?

Phillip.

Phillip who?

Phillip my bag with Halloween treats, please!

SPOOKY JOKES FOR FUNNY KIDS

What do you get when you drop a jack-o'-lantern from the roof?

Squash.

Why did the monsters eat all the party food?

They thought it was eerie-sistible.

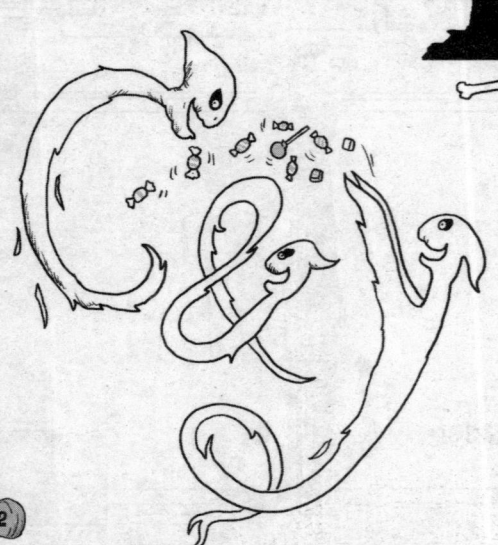

How do you spell candy with only two letters?

C and Y.

SPOOKY JOKES FOR FUNNY KIDS

Why did the witch's cat always stay in on Halloween?

Because it was a scaredy cat.

What do you get if you cross a vampire and a hot dog?

A fangfurter.

Why was the cemetery so busy on Halloween?

People were dying to get in.

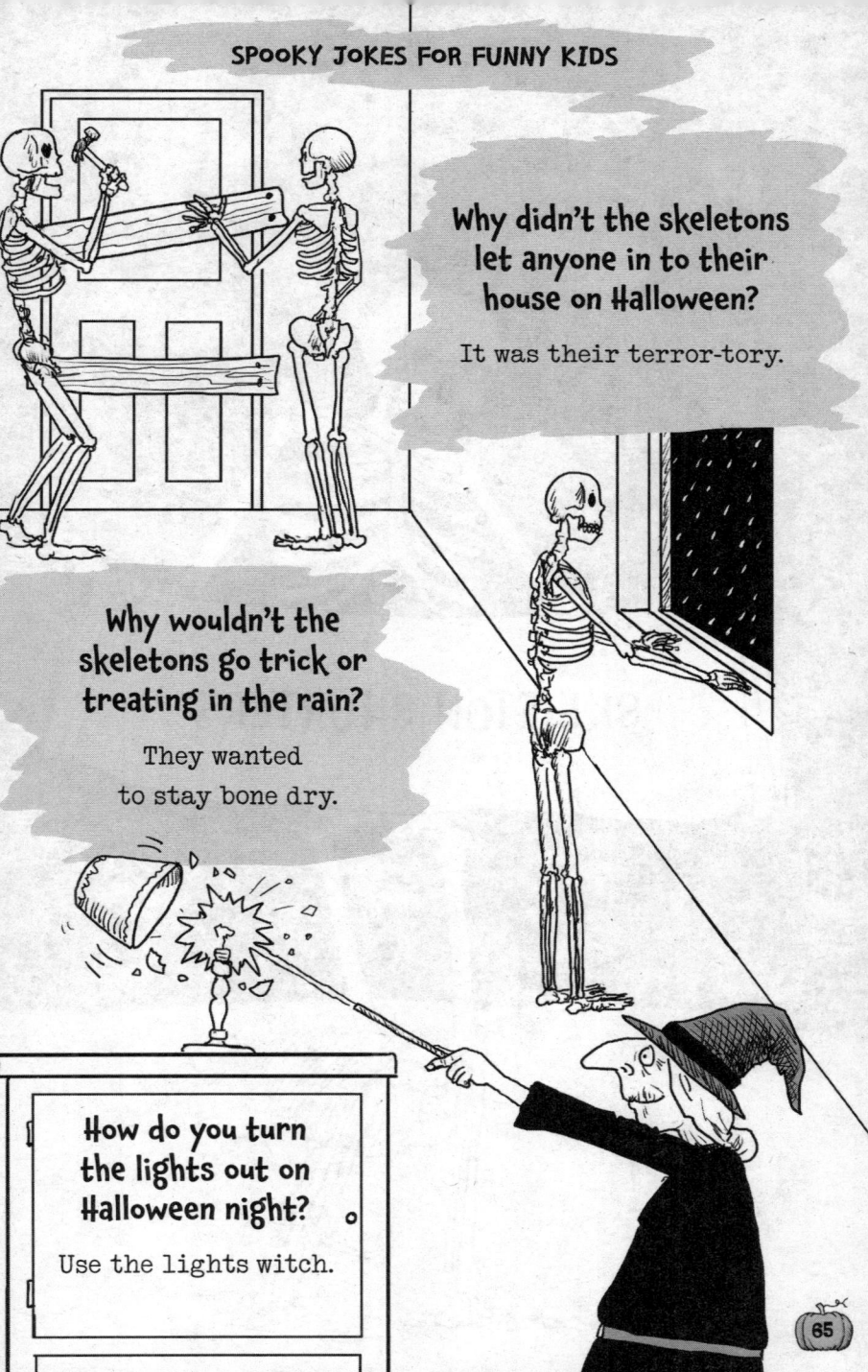

SPOOKY JOKES FOR FUNNY KIDS

What do you call a skeleton that never does any chores?

Lazy bones.

What do you call a shivering skeleton?

Numb-skull.

Why was the bone collector always busy?

She had a skele-TON of work to do.

SPOOKY JOKES FOR FUNNY KIDS

Why are skeletons so calm?

Because nothing gets under their skin.

Who is the most famous French skeleton?

Napoleon Bone-apart.

How do French skeletons say hello?

Bone-jour.

SPOOKY JOKES FOR FUNNY KIDS

Why did the skeleton have so many arguments?

She always had a bone to pick with someone.

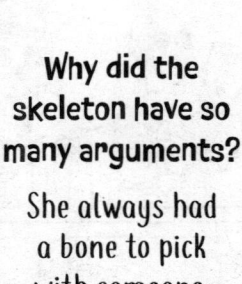

What did the skeleton do when he was cross?

Skull-ked a lot.

How can you cheer a skeleton up?

Tickle his funny bone.

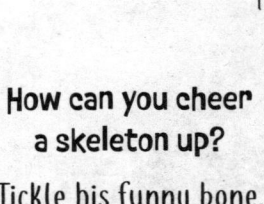

Tee-hee!

SPOOKY JOKES FOR FUNNY KIDS

Who won the skeleton beauty contest?
No-body.

What do you call a skeleton who solves mysteries?
Sherlock Bones.

What do you call a skeleton with no friends?
Bonely.

SPOOKY JOKES FOR FUNNY KIDS

What did the skeleton make in art class?

A skull-ture.

Why was the skeleton elected president?

She was a natural bone leader.

Why are skeletons so popular?

They always lend a hand.

Why couldn't the skeleton get out of bed?

He was bone tired.

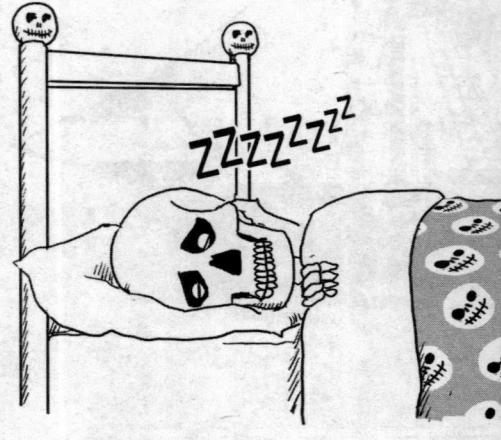

How did the skeleton look after working out at the gym?

Skele-toned.

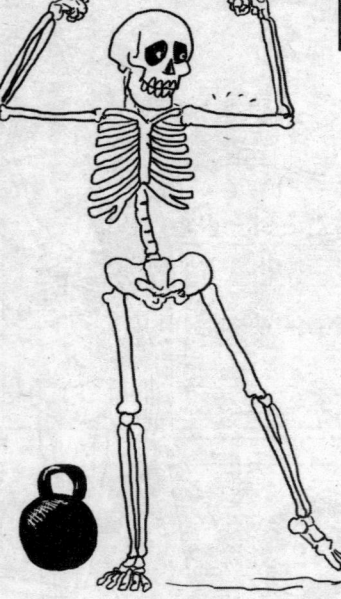

What do you call the skeleton who looks after everyone at the skeleton prom?

A chaper-bone.

SPOOKY JOKES FOR FUNNY KIDS

Why was the skeleton teacher cross with her pupil?

He was bone idle.

Why did the skeleton drop out of medical school?

Her heart wasn't in it.

Why couldn't the skeleton make any friends?

She had no social skulls.

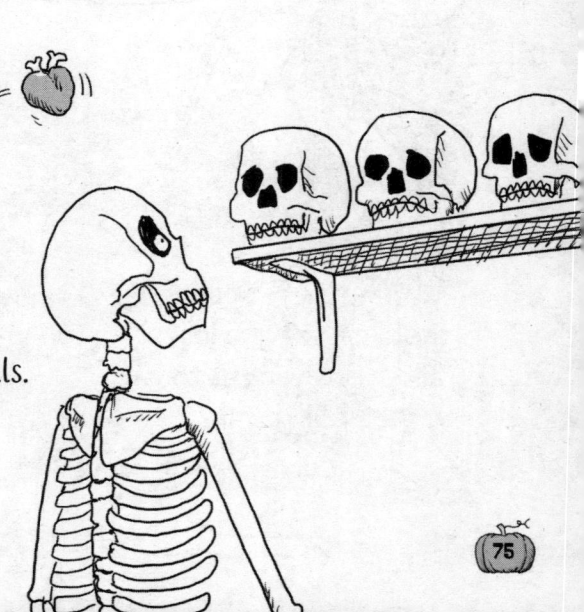

SPOOKY JOKES FOR FUNNY KIDS

How do monsters travel when they go abroad?

By scare-plane.

What do monsters use to cool down when they reach their hotel?

The scare-conditioner.

What do monsters eat when swimming in the sea?

Fish and ships.

SPOOKY JOKES FOR FUNNY KIDS

Why do vampires make terrible comedians?

Their jokes always suck!

Why do vampires enjoy thick books?

They love something they can get their teeth into.

How did the vampire describe the moment she first met her husband?

"It was love at first bite!"

What do you call a wolf who's always on the lookout?

Aware wolf.

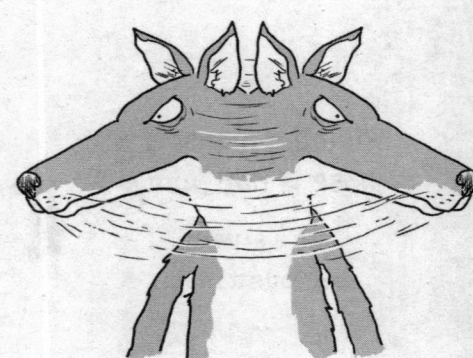

What do you call a singing monster with lots of fans?

A mon-star!

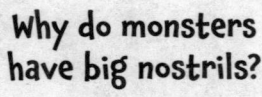

Why do monsters have big nostrils?

Because they have big fingers.

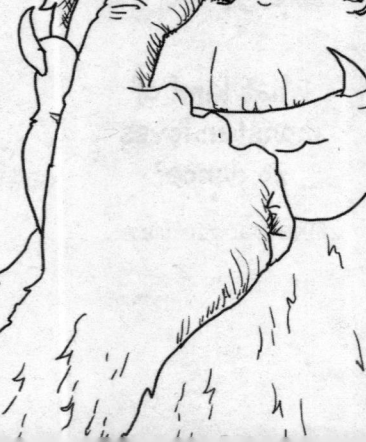

SPOOKY JOKES FOR FUNNY KIDS

What do you call a vampire that always wins at cards?

Dracu-luck.

Which vampire always eats junk food?

Snack-ula.

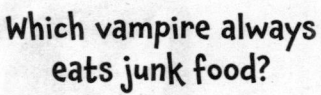

What did the vampire doctor shout out to the patients in her waiting room?

Necks, please!

SPOOKY JOKES FOR FUNNY KIDS

Who is the brightest monster?

Franken-shine.

What do you call a monster with great manners?

Thank-enstein.

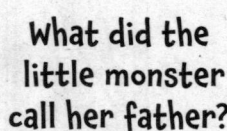

What did the little monster call her father?

Dead-y.

SPOOKY JOKES FOR FUNNY KIDS

Why didn't the monster want to go sky-diving?

He thought it would be a terror-flying experience.

Where do you find a monster snail?

At the end of a monster's finger.

Did you hear about the zombie that composed a symphony?

It was a monster-piece.

SPOOKY JOKES FOR FUNNY KIDS

What is the best way to reach the attic in a haunted house?

The mon-stairs.

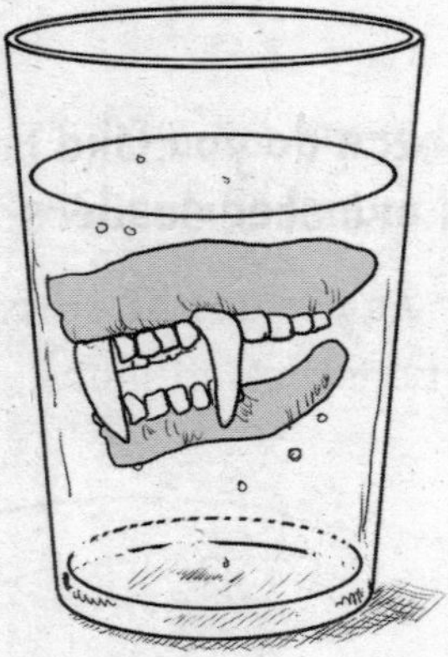

Why are vampires like false teeth?

Because they only come out at night.

Why was the mummy so tense?

He was all wound up.

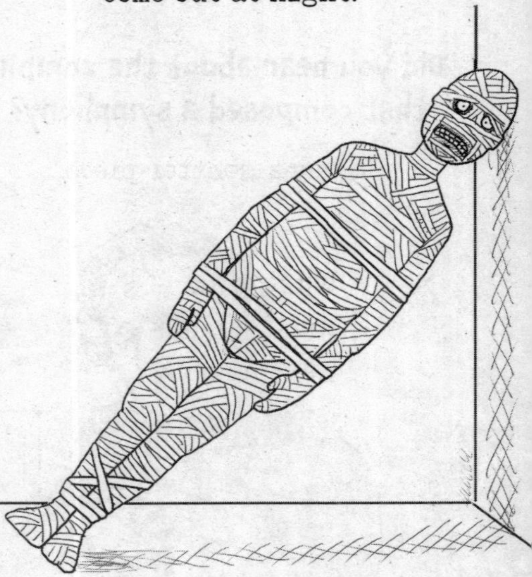

SPOOKY JOKES FOR FUNNY KIDS

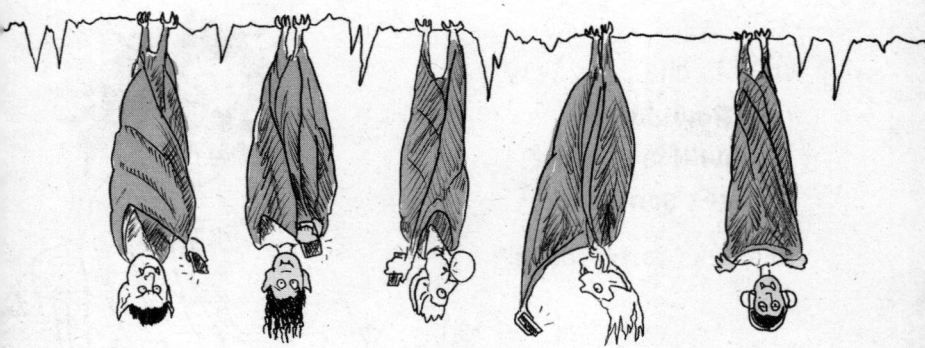

Why did the teenage vampires go into a cave?

Because they wanted to hang out.

Why do ghouls make the best cheerleaders?

They have a lot of spirit.

What kind of monster has the best hearing?

The eeriest.

SPOOKY JOKES FOR FUNNY KIDS

How do you know if a zombie likes someone?

She asks for seconds.

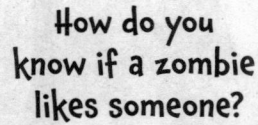

Why did the zombie become a musician?

He wanted to decompose some tunes.

What breed of dog does a zombie like best?

A ghoul-den retriever.

SPOOKY JOKES FOR FUNNY KIDS

Why don't witches like coffee shops?

They prefer to brew their own.

Where do werewolves keep their Halloween treats?

In a were-house.

Where do fleas go in winter?

Search me.

SPOOKY JOKES FOR FUNNY KIDS

What does a ghost call a mistake?

A BOO-BOO.

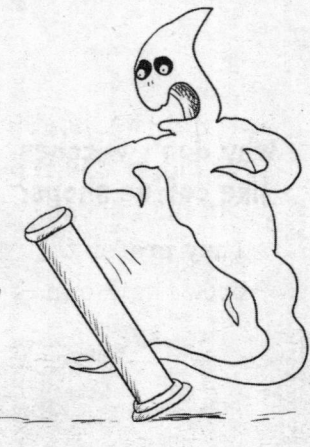

Why did the witch go to the hospital?

She had a dizzy spell.

Why do monsters always believe their horror-scopes?

They're ghoul-ible.

SPOOKY JOKES FOR FUNNY KIDS

How did the vampire get rid of the frog in his throat?

By coffin.

Why are werewolf parties so popular?

They're always a howling success.

Who won the zombie war?

Nobody, it was a dead heat.

SPOOKY JOKES FOR FUNNY KIDS

Why are zombies so clever?

They eat lots of brain food.

What comes from outer space and performs magic tricks?

A flying sorcerer.

What kind of TV do you find in a monster's house?

A wide-scream one.

SPOOKY JOKES FOR FUNNY KIDS

Knock, knock!
Who's there?
Witch.
Witch who?
Witch one of you can fix my broomstick?

Knock, knock!
Who's there?
Wanda.
Wanda who?
Wanda go for a ride on my broomstick?

Knock, knock!
Who's there?
Ice cream.
Ice cream who?
Ice cream every time I see a ghost.

SPOOKY JOKES FOR FUNNY KIDS

Knock, knock!
Who's there?
Disguise.
Disguise who?
Disguise dressed up like a monster for Halloween.

Knock, knock!
Who's there?
Bee.
Bee who?
Bee-ware, there's a full moon this Halloween.

Knock, knock!
Who's there?
Witches.
Witches who?
Witches the way to the haunted house?

Knock, knock!
Who's there?
Tyson.
Tyson who?
Tyson garlic around your neck to ward off vampires.

Knock, knock!
Who's there?
Ghost.
Ghost who?
Ghost stand over there and I'll bring you some treats.

Knock, knock!
Who's there?
Viper.
Viper who?
Viper your mouth when you're done sucking blood.

SPOOKY JOKES FOR FUNNY KIDS

Knock, knock!
Who's there?
Wooden shoe.
Wooden shoe who?
Wooden shoe like to give me some Halloween treats?

Knock, knock!
Who's there?
Armageddon.
Armageddon who?
Armageddon out of here – this graveyard is haunted!

Knock, knock!
Who's there?
Noah.
Noah who?
Noah place I can hide from ghosts?

Knock, knock!
Who's there?
Handsome.
Handsome who?
Handsome Halloween treats to me.

Knock, knock!
Who's there?
Felix.
Felix who?
Felix-cited about Halloween.

Knock, knock!
Who's there?
Eva.
Eva who?
Eva seen a werewolf?

SPOOKY JOKES FOR FUNNY KIDS

Knock, knock!
Who's there?
Ben.
Ben who?
Ben waiting for Halloween all year.

Knock, knock!
Who's there?
Orange.
Orange who?
Orange you glad I'm just a pumpkin and not a monster?

Knock, knock!
Who's there?
Yeti.
Yeti who?
Yeti or not, here I come!

SPOOKY JOKES FOR FUNNY KIDS

Knock, knock.
Who's there?
Ivana.
Ivana who?
Ivana suck your blood.

Knock, knock.
Who's there?
Grave.
Grave who?
Grave mistake, never open your door to a zombie!

Knock, knock.
Who's there?
Howl!
Howl who?
Howl you know unless you open the door?

SPOOKY JOKES FOR FUNNY KIDS

Knock, knock.
Who's there?
Police.
Police who?
Police let me in, there's a monster chasing me!

Knock, knock!
Who's there?
Alison.
Alison who?
Alison out carefully for werewolves on Halloween.

Knock, knock!
Who's there?
Juan.
Juan who?
Juan-eyed monster.

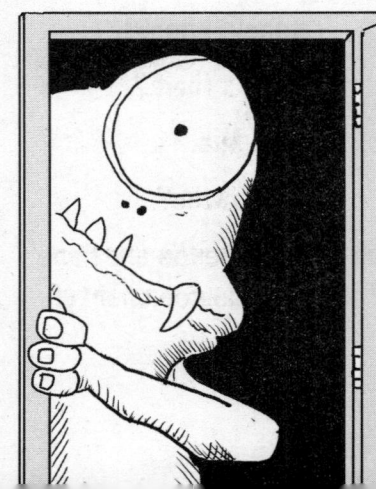

Knock, knock.
Who's there?
Olive.
Olive who?
Olive Halloween.

Knock, knock.
Who's there?
Terry.
Terry who?
Terry-fied of ghosts and ghouls, let me in!

Knock, knock!
Who's there?
Mia.
Mia who?
Mia-nd my friends are here for the Halloween party!

SPOOKY JOKES FOR FUNNY KIDS

What do you call a pile of black cats?

A meow-tain.

What do black cats love to eat?

Paw-sta.

Which dessert do witches give their cats?

Mice-cream.

SPOOKY JOKES FOR FUNNY KIDS

Why are black cats good singers?

Because they're mew-sical.

Why did the witch have a headache?

Because her cat loved playing purr-cussion.

Where does the witch always take her cat for a treat?

The mew-seum.

SPOOKY JOKES FOR FUNNY KIDS

What do you get when you cross a black cat with a witch's rug?

A magic car-pet.

What happened when the black cat forgot Halloween?

It was a cat-astrophe!

What did the black cat say when its friend ate all the Halloween treats?

SPOOKY JOKES FOR FUNNY KIDS

SPOOKY JOKES FOR FUNNY KIDS

What do you call a witch with a frog on her head?

Lily.

Why did the frog go to the hospital?

It needed a hopperation.

What do stylish frogs wear?

Jumpsuits.

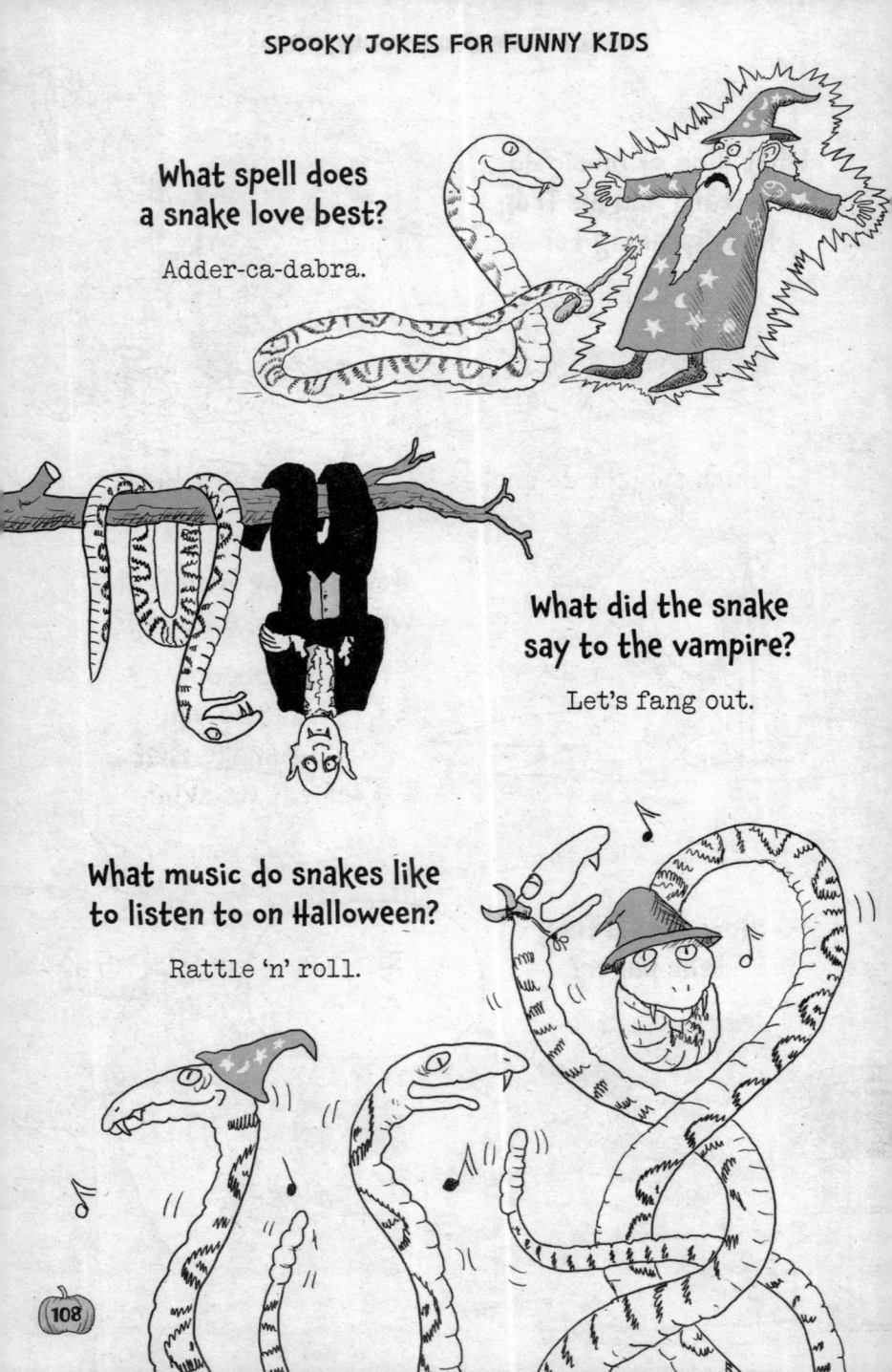

SPOOKY JOKES FOR FUNNY KIDS

Which subject do snakes love to study at school?

Hisss-tory.

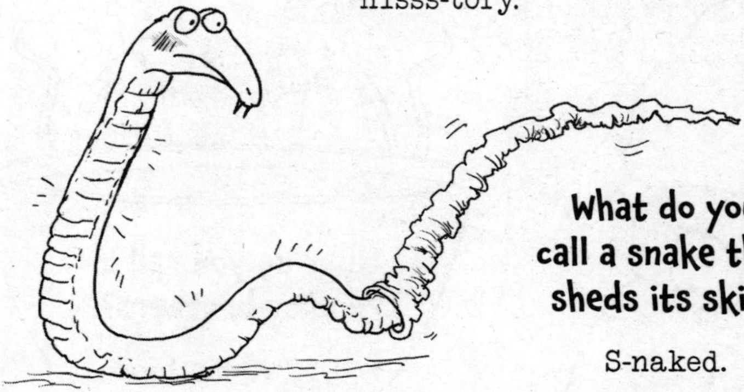

What do you call a snake that sheds its skin?

S-naked.

What do you call a snake that builds things?

A boa constructor.

SPOOKY JOKES FOR FUNNY KIDS

What do you call two mice in love?

Squeakhearts.

What do you call two mice brothers?

Bro-dents.

Why wouldn't the mouse tell the witch its name?

It preferred to stay anony-mouse.

SPOOKY JOKES FOR FUNNY KIDS

Which martial art are rats best at?

Ka-rat-e.

How do you get a rat to smile?

Tell it some cheesy jokes.

What do you call a rat who sails around looking for treasure?

A pi-rat.

SPOOKY JOKES FOR FUNNY KIDS

What do little bats learn at school?

The alpha-bat.

Where do bats carry their school books?

In their bat-packs.

What do you call a bat that cheats in tests?

A copy-bat.

SPOOKY JOKES FOR FUNNY KIDS

Why was the witch cross with her bat?

She thought it was bat tempered.

Why did the wizard decide against a bat for a pet?

He thought it was a bat idea.

Which sport do bats love to play?

Bat-minton.

SPOOKY JOKES FOR FUNNY KIDS

What do you call two spiders who just got married?

Newly-webbeds.

Why did the spider go to computer college?

It wanted to become a web designer.

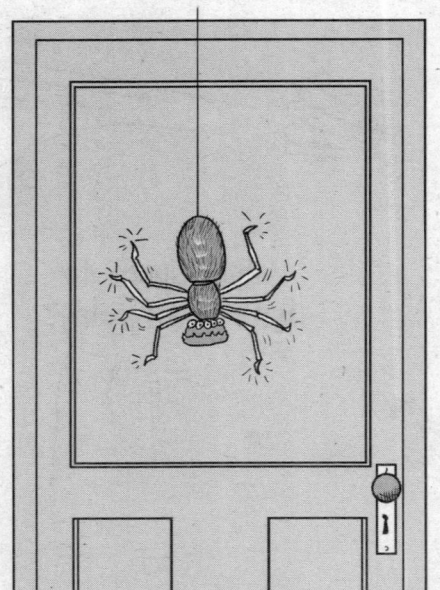

Knock,
knock,
knock,
knock,
knock,
knock,
knock,
knock.

Who's there?

A spider.

SPOOKY JOKES FOR FUNNY KIDS

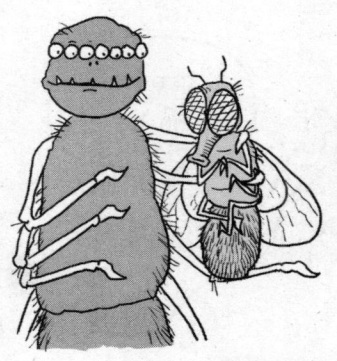

Why was the friendly spider always hungry?

Because it wouldn't hurt a fly.

What do spiders eat in Paris?

French flies.

Why should you stay inside when it's raining spiders?

To avoid getting caught in a tarantula downpour.

SPOOKY JOKES FOR FUNNY KIDS

Why is the air so clean when there's a full moon?

Because witches sweep the sky.

What do Australian ghosts love to play with?

BOO-merangs!

Why was there no food left at the end of the monster's party?

Because everyone was a goblin.

SPOOKY JOKES FOR FUNNY KIDS

Why do witches dislike winter?

Too many cold spells.

What game does a monster love best?

Swallow the leader.

Why are mummies so good at keeping secrets?

Because they can keep things under wraps.

SPOOKY JOKES FOR FUNNY KIDS

What did the witch do when she wanted to become fitter?

Hex-ercise.

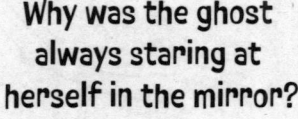

Why was the ghost always staring at herself in the mirror?

She thought she was BOO-tiful.

What do you get when you cross a vampire and a teacher?

Lots of blood tests.

SPOOKY JOKES FOR FUNNY KIDS

How does a vampire like his food served?

In bite-size portions.

What did the ghost monkey love to eat?

BOO-nanas.

What's another name for a witch's garage?

A broom closet.

SPOOKY JOKES FOR FUNNY KIDS

Which nursery rhyme do baby ghosts love best?

Little BOO-peep.

What kind of music do ghosts love?

Soul music.

Why do ghosts hate walking?

They're always dead on their feet.

SPOOKY JOKES FOR FUNNY KIDS

What do you call a lost wolf?

A where-wolf.

Which celebration do werewolves love best?

Howl-oween.

What do ghosts love to do at the gym?

Dead lifts.

SPOOKY JOKES FOR FUNNY KIDS

What do you call an owl that can make itself disappear?

Hoot-dini.

What do you call a magician who has lost his magic?

Ian.

Why was the wizard so good at sums?

He was a brilliant mathemagician.

SPOOKY JOKES FOR FUNNY KIDS

Who keeps zombies, ghouls and monsters safe at the beach?

The Ghost Guard.

What's another word for a baby ghost?

A handkerchief.

Why do mummies make the best detectives?

They're great at unravelling mysteries.

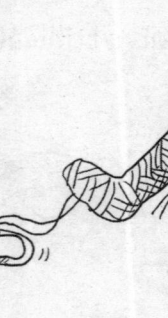

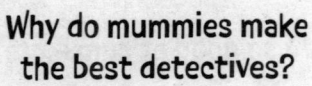

SPOOKY JOKES FOR FUNNY KIDS

What do you call a vampire that lives in the kitchen?

Count Spatula.

What did the witch say when her friend married a ghost?

I don't know what possessed her!

Why did the ghost cross the road?

To get to the 'other side'.

ALSO AVAILABLE: